Beauty for Ashes

Freedom from the Wrong Touch

Delvia Y. Berrian

Barlow Enterprises, LLC
Cheltenham, PA

Copyright ©2020 by Press for Kingdom Living, LLC. All rights reserved. No portion of this book may be reproduced, stored in a retrieval system, or transmitted by any means, mechanical, electronic, photocopying, recording, or otherwise—without the prior written permission of the author.

SBN: 978-1-7349439-0-0 Library of Congress Cataloging-in-Publication Date is available.

Project Specialist/Author Coach
Barlow Enterprises, LLC
Write Your Book Now! Visit: www.destinystatement.com or Text 478-227-5692

Legal Disclaimer

While none of the stories in this book are fabricated, some of the names and details may have been changed to protect the privacy of the individuals mentioned. Although the author and publisher have made every effort to ensure that the information in this book was correct at time of press, the author and publisher do not assume and hereby disclaim any liability to any party for any loss, damage, or disruption caused by errors or omissions, whether such errors or omissions result from negligence, accident, or any other cause.

Ordering Information

Beauty for Ashes may be purchased in large quantities at a discount for educational, business, or sales promotional use. For more information or to request Ms. Delvia Berrian as the speaker at your next event email: beautyforashes520@gmail.com

Praise for Beauty for Ashes

This book is a powerful and profound statement of a life transformed. It is an honest and sincere reflection of triumph over trouble. It demonstrates that no matter where you start out, God can take you to your mountain top. This book should be read by all young people, but especially by those who have suffered trauma in their lives. I recommend it for all youth workers and counselors of all ages. This book is a gift to all who are seeking to overcome hardships and adversity.

I also strongly recommend this book for social workers, ministers, and teachers at all levels. Reading *Beauty for Ashes: Freedom from the Wrong Touch*, will help professionals who deal with trauma to understand the journey of those with whom they are working. This is a must-read book.

~ The Honorable Rev. Dr. W. Wilson Goode, Sr.

Beauty for Ashes: Freedom from the Wrong Touch is a great contribution to the literature on trauma. It will undoubtedly benefit many. In her transparency, Ms. Berrian reveals how unforgiveness seemingly does not impact the perpetrator but imprisons the victim in detrimental emotional cycles. She uses her relationship with God to show us how to find love for self which ultimately enables us to forgive and which helps to eradicate many of the conditions and emotions that torment those in trauma. Ms. Berrian offers hope by mapping out a path for the hurt child within to experience the joy of fulfilling their destiny beyond the ashes.

~ Christi Sanders, MA

Delvia Berrian has great spiritual insight and first-hand experience in surviving trauma. She is a woman pursuing the call of God.

By paralleling her life experience with relevant scripture, she shows us how to deal with trauma head-on by welcoming God in the healing process. Ms. Berrian has created a powerful method for serious, sustainable freedom from past hurts, shame and trauma.

Read this book. You'll find it difficult to dispute her view that, as Christians, we must serve as models to this hurting world, that Jesus is the light, the truth and the way for us all.

~ Minister Brent Brickley

The last chapter of Beauty for Ashes, entitled, A Trauma Worker's Survival Guide, provides resourceful, informative and relatable practice approaches for novice and advanced social work professional alike. Clear and common place examples provide easy to understand intervention modalities rooted in empirical practices across all service strata.

The author has mastered the infusion of clinical social work theory, functional service provision models and a Christ center delivery method. Chapter 11 of this book, A Trauma Worker's Survival Guide, is a must read for youth entering the service field, as well as, for professionals with decades of service to diverse client populations. There is something fresh, relatable and exciting for everyone!

~ Zachary S. Harris, MSA, MSW, LSW

Dedication

This book is dedicated to the person who has experienced childhood trauma and is struggling to find their way.

Foreword

Trauma has a profound impact on its victims. It is even more detrimental to growth and development, when it occurs in childhood. It has the potential to leave deeply embedded scars that, if left untreated, fester and spill over into adult life. Inevitably, unaddressed trauma negatively impacts the victim's social, emotional, physical and spiritual well-being. Consequently, trauma *must* be addressed, so that those who are affected can heal in safe, holistic ways. Delvia Berrian's transparent, heartfelt memoir demonstrates that she has done exactly that! Delvia dives into the most vulnerable parts of herself. She reflects and tells her story in a unique and relatable way. I was drawn into the book within the first few minutes of picking it up. You will be too.

The author bares her soul. She tells her very private story, so that others can overcome their traumatic experiences, heal and serve others, just like she has. She pours out her innermost feelings and reveals her anxieties, setbacks and failures. However, Ms. Berrian does not stop there! She does not simply tell her story. She reveals the effective, proven methods that she used to overcome the social, emotional, physical and spiritual issues of her past -- issues which could have had serious implications on her growth and development. However, once it became apparent to her that she would remain stuck if she did not seek godly wisdom, she did the hard work that is required to shift from the desolation of trauma's ashes into God's brilliance and beauty.

Ms. Berrian concludes the book by providing the reader a glimpse of how her life has evolved once she allowed God and a professional therapist to help her transform her life. *Beauty for Ashes* allows you to experience Ms. Berrian's transformation. She risks sharing closely held personal secrets, so that we be transformed too. Much hope will be gained, as you read this strong, resilient woman's story.

Anita C. Gregory, PhD
Doctor of Philosophy in Organizational Leadership

Free to Let Go

Lord, how long will my past haunt me? Lord, I want to be free

I want to be free of the pain

I want to be free of the hurt

I want to be free of the shame

How long, Lord, do I have to struggle with the residue?

Oh, wow! I thought I turned it over to you

Lord, I hear you telling me to let it go

But, Lord, pain, hurt and shame is all I know

Shape me, mold me, Lord, to be a whole and not a half

I know I have to let go of my past and follow your path

I thought I was free, but my past keeps bothering me

What is it I must confront? Why is this overwhelming me?

I truly need to be healed by Thee

Is there resentment inside of me?

Help me, Lord!

I really want the victory!

Are you there, God? It's me

Please reveal yourself to me

I want to be free, bold, powerful

and used by you to break the mold

Reveal, Lord — must my story be told?

I am chasing after you, Lord

Please tell me what to do

Contents

Part I Path of Pain

The History of Trauma 1
My Story 13
The Year of Manifestation 19
The Year of Revelation 25

Part II Road to Recovery

Allow the Triune God into Your Situation 31
Forgiveness 41
Transform Your Mind 49
Reflect to Stay on Track 56
Walk in Purpose 64
Keep a Journal 68

Part III A Trauma Workers Survival Guide

A Trauma Workers Survival Guide 81

Introduction

Cast all your anxiety on Him because He cares for you.

~ 1 Peter 5:7

Trauma causes stress on the body. It is emotionally and psychologically disturbing. Trauma is difficult for the person who suffers from its impact.

Trauma can be caused by a variety of things including gun violence, rape, pain, grief, military combat and sexual, physical or emotional abuse. There are clearly vast and varying degrees of incidents that can cause trauma.

Physical trauma often heals. The trauma may leave a small scar or some other visible trace of the fact that pain was inflicted, but eventually the scar heals. Sometimes, there is minimal evidence that we were wounded at all. Nonetheless, we must not let the absence of physical scars to deceive us. The sociopsychological effects of trauma can be difficult to detect. Emotional and psychological scarring present differently. It is manifested through behaviors that are detrimental to the traumatized person's state of mind. It is not unusual for people who are traumatized to feel guilt, shame, blame, anger and low self-esteem. These are all emotions that people in trauma often work through, by exhibiting destructive behavior. Destructive behaviors can include eating disorders, sleep disorders, sexual dysfunction, drug addiction, depression, anxiety, dissociative states, repeated self-injury, suicide attempts, lying, stealing, truancy, running away, poor contraceptive practices, compulsive sexual behaviors, and intolerance of or a constant search for intimacy. When these behaviors manifest from trauma they can, and often do evolve into vicious cycles of self-inflicted pain of one form or another, because trauma unchecked, leads to more trauma.

In my trauma-focused practice, I have found that trauma is a subject about which many people – professional and clients -- disagree when it comes to how to handle and treat it. Some schools of thought believe that the best way to handle trauma is to do the difficult work that is necessary to face and overcome the trauma, so that it does not haunt the person for the rest of their life. On the other hand, some people approach trauma timidly. They think that avoiding the fact that they are in distress will make it go away.

In the process of doing the work to heal my own trauma and then helping others to do the same, I designed a clinically proven method that enables those who are struggling, with how to move beyond the trauma they have endured. I have named it the Come Out of the Ashes© Program.

We try to forget some traumatic experiences, because they are just so unspeakable. However, those painful experiences should not and cannot be buried. This is precisely why the pain of our traumas, no matter how well we thought we had buried them, so often resurrects, haunts and eventually drives us to self-destruct. These self-destructive behaviors show up in the form of addiction, promiscuity, obesity and low self-esteem. Most often they are not realized or resolved, until the trauma is addressed in a therapeutic setting. These behaviors are used to mask the hurt, pain, guilt and shame of the trauma. In order to heal from trauma, the root or cause must be discovered and explored. Most people do not want to relive the past, they want to suppress it. Church goers are told to forget the things from the past. We cannot, however, move forward as healthy and whole individuals, until we address what happened to us.

The purpose of this book is threefold. First, it is written so that I can tell my story of overcoming trauma. The apostle Paul tells us in Philippians 3:13-14 to forget the things that are behind. He writes:

> *Brothers, I do not consider myself yet to have taken hold of it. But one thing I do: Forgetting what is behind and straining toward what is ahead, I press on toward the goal to win the prize for which God has called me heavenward in Christ Jesus.*

When we study the text, the apostle Paul did not mean that we are to bury our hurts, betrayals, rapes, murders, or any other hideous acts we may have survived and placed behind us. No! Paul is speaking about the past blessings of God. Paul is telling us to make God's aim, our aim. He is challenging us to look for new mercies and new blessings daily so that we do not get stuck on what God did in the past. Some have interpreted this scripture to mean that you should forget what happened to you as a child, but that interpretation contradicts the healing process. In order to heal from our past, we must acknowledge and remember it.

My second purpose in writing Beauty for Ashes is to discuss why we cannot move forward, until we address what is behind us. It has been said that time heals all wounds. This is another myth that can hinder the healing process. We cannot forget the past or expect time to heal hurt, pain, or betrayal. We must confront the past. Any kind of trauma, when left unchecked, suppressed, or covered up, will bleed into the future. I can think of many instances, where my failure to settle myself and do the work that was necessary to heal from my past negatively affected my new relationships. I was unable to trust or allow people to get close to me, because I still carried so much fear. I was abused. As a result, I viewed everyone as if they would eventually violate and cause me pain.

We must heal from all past hurt and not allow the past to affect or infect our future. I sometimes think of all the relationships and opportunities I missed, because of my unchecked trauma. I don't get stuck on the missed opportunities and the damage I caused to myself. I let it go! Because we never know how our actions affect others, I also asked for forgiveness for the damage I may have caused others.

The third and final purpose of this book is to share the Come Out of the Ashes© process that I used to overcome trauma and to share some of what I have come to see as best practices or approaches, when it comes to helping professionals to guide their clients through healing from trauma. If I were to rewrite the scripture mentioned above, I would say,

Brothers and sisters, I have not achieved all that God has for me, but I do know one thing: I will address every past hurt, trauma, and betrayal in a healthy, therapeutic way! I will not harbor ill will toward myself or anyone who have hurt or offended me in any way. I will move ahead with God!

I cannot emphasize this point enough. The only way to heal trauma, is to address it head-on. We make the most progress when dealing with trauma, when we decide to unpack every level of it. The trauma and pain must be properly processed in order to identify the triggers. Only then, can we prevent the constant cycles of destruction that occur when trauma is ignored.

Although I used the methods that I will teach you to heal from sexual abuse, I have found that these methods are both applicable and effective for use in addressing other traumatic or hurtful experiences.

Part I

Path of Pain

Chapter 1

The History of Trauma

Trauma has been around since the fall of humankind in the garden of Eden. The Bible is full of traumatic stories. The first murder was traumatic. Abel killed his brother Cain. Joseph faced several traumatic events in his life. He was thrown into a pit, imprisoned and lied about by Potiphar's wife. That is traumatic. Jesus' death by crucifixion was beyond traumatic. The hateful stoning of Stephen, the relentless persecution of Christians and the torture and imprisonment of so many of the apostles was traumatic.

Times have changed, but people still endure unfathomably difficult situations. We live in an imperfect world and are caused pain due to jealousy, lust, envy, and racism. Some people are hated solely because of their religious beliefs. As a society we are now bombarded with mass shootings, and all sorts of terrorism (both domestic and abroad). Trauma continues to plague our world.

Tamar's Trauma

A most horrific act was experienced in King David's family. Although King David was known as a mighty warrior, who unified the twelve tribes of Israel, he was also known for his many lustful acts. He had Uriah the Hittite killed because he wanted Bathsheba, Uriah's wife, for himself. This same trickery plagued his son Amnon, who became so obsessed with his half-sister, Tamar that he became physically sick. In 2 Samuel 13, we learn of Amnon's deceitful ways and see how his obsession created a whirlwind of casualties:

Some time passed. David's son Absalom had a beautiful sister whose name was Tamar; and David's son Amnon fell in love with her. Amnon was so tormented that he made himself ill because of his sister Tamar, for she was a virgin and it seemed impossible to Amnon to do anything to her. But Amnon had a friend whose name was Jonadab, the son of David's brother Shimeah; and Jonadab was a very crafty man. He said to him, "O son of the king, why are you so haggard morning after morning? Will you not tell me?" Amnon said to him, "I love Tamar, my brother Absalom's sister." Jonadab said to him, "Lie down on your bed, and pretend to be ill; and when your father comes to see you, say to him, 'Let my sister Tamar come and give me something to eat, and prepare the food in my sight, so that I may see it and eat it from her hand.'" So Amnon lay down and pretended to be ill; and when the king came to see him, Amnon said to the king, "Please let my sister Tamar come and make a couple of cakes in my sight, so that I may eat from her hand." Then David sent home to Tamar, saying, "Go to your brother Amnon's house, and prepare food for him." So Tamar went to her brother Amnon's house, where he was lying down. She took dough, kneaded it, made cakes in his sight, and baked the cakes. Then she took the pan and set them out before him, but he refused to eat. Amnon said, "Send out everyone from me." So everyone went out from him. Then Amnon said to Tamar, "Bring the food into the chamber, so that I may eat from your hand." So Tamar took the cakes she had made and brought them into the chamber to Amnon her brother. But when she brought them near him to eat, he took hold of her, and said to her, "Come, lie with me, my sister." She answered him, "No, my brother, do not force me; for such a thing is not done in Israel; do not do anything so vile! As for me, where could I carry my shame? And as for you, you would be as one of the scoundrels in Israel. Now therefore, I beg you, speak to the king; for he will not withhold me from you." But he would not listen to her; and being stronger than she, he forced her and lay with her.

Then Amnon was seized with a very great loathing for her; indeed, his loathing was even greater than the lust he had felt for her. Amnon said to her, "Get out!" But she said to him, "No, my brother; for this wrong in sending me away is greater than the other that you did to me." But he would not listen to her. He called the young man who served him and said, "Put this woman out of my presence, and bolt the door after her." (Now she was wearing a long robe with sleeves; for this is how the virgin daughters of the king were clothed in earlier times.) So his servant put her out and bolted the door after her. But Tamar put ashes on her head and tore the long robe that she was wearing; she put her hand on her head, and went away, crying aloud as she went.

> Her brother Absalom said to her, "Has Amnon your brother been with you? Be quiet for now, my sister; he is your brother; do not take this to heart." So Tamar remained, a desolate woman, in her brother Absalom's house. When King David heard of all these things, he became very angry, but he would not punish his son Amnon, because he loved him, for he was his firstborn. But Absalom spoke to Amnon neither good nor bad; for Absalom hated Amnon, because he had raped his sister Tamar.

Amnon's lustful act in this story, results in traumatizing a number of people in the family. Absalom becomes so enraged that he plots to kill Amnon. However, his rage does not end with Amnon. He is very upset with his father, King David for not addressing Amnon's behavior. As a result, Absalom goes after his father's kingdom, which leads to his death. Tamar's life was ruined. She became a desolate woman, disgraced, shamed and never to marry, because of Amnon's egregious act. Absalom was trying to protect and be there for his sister but minimized

Tamar's feelings when he told her. "Don't take heart." King David was angry about Amnon's actions. However, he loved him, and he did not discipline him, which further victimized Tamar. Trauma stopped Tamar from living the type of life she would have lived, if her virginity had not been taken by her brother or had he married her after he raped her. More than likely, she lived the remainder of her life in a royal harem, because that is where virgin girls lived until they were married. Unfortunately, what became of Tamar's life after rape was not deemed important enough to be included in the Bible. Despite her royal status, women were still considered property. This is actually the same attitude we have towards women who are victims of sexual abuse today. Society at large says, like Absalom did to Tamar, "Go somewhere and don't take the violation of your body to heart. You knew what you were going to his room to do." We still hear this sentiment today from people who do not support the Me-Too movement. King David's decision not to justly respond and hold his son accountable, left Tamar exposed, unprotected and uncovered. He protected his son – the rapist – but the king did nothing to vindicate his daughter – the victim. It is a fact that King David's family could not shake the demons that surrounded them. If we go back to the king's lineage, there is story after story of deceitful behavior. Unfortunately, generations of abuse are often found in the family histories of children who are abused. The parents are sometimes victims of abuse themselves or are so dependent on the abuser, that they do not defend their helpless children because they cannot see their lives without the abuser.

Joseph's Trauma

Let's look at another Biblical example. Joseph suffered tremendous trauma throughout his life, beginning with the jealousy of his brothers because of his dreams. He was thrown into a pit, he was a slave, he was lied about by Potiphar's wife and he unjustly spent time in prison. Joseph and Tamar suffered physical, mental and emotional trauma. The trauma Joseph faced in his life did not stop God from keeping the promises that God made to Joseph in his dreams. Joseph responded to his suffering with faith and humility. Joseph could have easily become bitter, but instead, he continued to trust God's plan and believed that he would see the visions that he was shown in his dreams come to past.

Job's Trauma

Tamar and Joseph were not the only people in the Old Testament who suffered tremendous trauma. Job suffered, and he was an upright man. God allowed Satan to attack Job, but He also kept a hedge around his life. As we see in Job chapter 1:6-12:

> One day the angels came to present themselves before the LORD, and satan also came with them. The LORD said to satan, "Where have you come from?" satan answered the LORD, "From roaming throughout the earth, going back and forth on it." Then the LORD said to Satan, "Have you considered my servant Job? There is no one on earth like him; he is blameless and upright, a man who fears God and shuns evil. "Does Job fear God for nothing?" Satan replied. 1"Have you not put a hedge around him and his household and

everything he has? You have blessed the work of his hands, so that his flocks and herds are spread throughout the land. But now stretch out your hand and strike everything he has, and he will surely curse you to your face. "The LORD said to Satan, "Very well, then, everything he has is in your power, but on the man, himself do not lay a finger. "Then Satan went out from the presence of the LORD.

God allowed satan to kill Job's cattle and children, burn down his house and inflict him with boils all over his body and yet, Job still revered God. Job was urged by his wife and three friends to curse God and die because of his intense sufferings. Job did not curse God, but he did question God about his suffering. When we experience unexplained trauma or unprovoked suffering, it is natural to question why God would allow such things to happen to undeserving people. God is just and powerful. At any time, He could have stopped Job's suffering. Knowing this would make anyone wonder, what's the purpose? Was God was trying to prove a point to satan? The message and point are clear. Satan can only do what God allows him to do. Throughout all of Job's trials and tribulations, he remained faithful to God. After learning that all his children died when a house collapsed on them, Job says:

> *Naked I came from my mother's womb,*
>
> *and naked I will depart.*
>
> *The LORD gave and the LORD has taken away;*
>
> *may the name of the LORD be praised.*
>
> *The Bible says, "In all this, Job did not sin by charging God with wrongdoing."*

Throughout the Book of Job, he converses with his three friends and he defends God. Job pleads his case and remains committed to God, while he suffers traumatic loss after traumatic loss. Like Joseph, after the trauma had ceased, Job was vindicated and rewarded by God for his faithfulness. In Job 42, the scripture tells us:

The LORD blessed the latter part of Job's life more than the former part. He had fourteen thousand sheep, six thousand camels, a thousand yoke of oxen and a thousand donkeys. And he also had seven sons and three daughters. The first daughter he named Jemimah, the second Keziah and the third Keren-Happuch. Nowhere in all the land were there found women as beautiful as Job's daughters, and their father granted them an inheritance along with their brothers. After this, Job lived a hundred and forty years; he saw his children and their children to the fourth generation. And so Job died, an old man and full of years.

Everything Job lost in the most treacherous and challenging seasons of his life was restored to him. As a matter of fact, when it was all over, he was blessed with much, much more.

Chapter 2

My Story

Before I formed you in the womb, I knew you. Before you were born, I set you apart; I appointed you as a prophet to the nations.
~ Jeremiah 1:5

This is my trauma story — this is my truth! When I was about eight years old, we abruptly moved to Germantown, because my mother had left my abusive adoptive father. Suddenly, due to domestic violence, she was now a single parent who had to provide for me and my siblings alone. To make ends meet, my mother took a job working at night in a twenty-four-hour laundromat, and we were left with a caregiver.

This was a very difficult time for me. I was mourning the loss of the familiar; and adjusting to my new normal: a new school, new house, new friends and a new routine. One of the most horrifying things happened to me when I was nine-years old. It was something that no child should have to experience.

It was a cold winter night. My siblings and I were all piled in the bed, as we sometimes did. We were all still uneasy because of the newness of our circumstances. It was difficult to sleep in the new setting. To make matters worse, every evening after my mother would leave for work, there was a party in our house. People were drinking, smoking and playing loud music. The house would eventually become quiet and I could feel the presence of someone in the room. The stench of alcohol, cigarettes and marijuana was very heavy. I was afraid to look up, because I didn't want to get in trouble for not being asleep. The nightly visits eventually led to the touching of my genitalia. I pretended as if I were sleeping and didn't realize what was going on. I was afraid to say anything to anyone, because I didn't want to get in trouble. Every night the room would become overwhelmed with the stench of cigarettes, alcohol and marijuana. To this day, this combination sickens me, because it reminds me of that tragic time in my childhood.

I grew up during an era when you didn't question authority. You stayed in a child's place, and what went on in your house, stayed in your house. The stares and touching of my genitalia eventually led to me being carried away one night. Isolated in another room, I could no longer pretend to be asleep. The touching and groping of my genitalia led to sexual intercourse. I was raped. I cried silently, afraid to make a noise, shocked by what was happening. My nine-year-old body was sore. I bled but was too afraid to tell anyone. I suffered in silence. I was in disbelief. I cried silently, afraid to tell anyone what happened, even my siblings.

The next day, it was business as usual. My mother went to work; our caregiver came and there was a party — loud music, smoking, and drinking.

This abuse continued for a little over three years. I was around twelve years old when it ended. It was never exposed. I put a stop to it by saying, "No more." I had developed the courage to say, "Stop! Enough of this nonsense." For three years, I endured painful violations and suffered in silence. This was not my only abuser. When a child is sexually abused, it marks them for other predators.

The closest I ever came to reveal what happened, was when I was in the sixth grade. There was a kid running around in the girls' bathroom, groping girls. I made up a story that this same kid also did this to me. However, it came out that I lied, because he wasn't in school the day. I said he touched me. The trouble I got in for that lie! My God, the whooping was unbelievable. I still remember it like yesterday. I lied right in front of the kid and his mother. Lord, forgive me because I never repented for that lie or apologized to the kid. I was condemned for lying about this kid, instead of someone having the wisdom to know that children don't just make up those kinds of stories without cause. When I reflect on my childhood, there were several times when I was crying out for help. I was disruptive in school, church, the neighborhood and in my family.

This disruptive behavior was my way of lashing out. I was very mean. As a matter fact, I became a bully. I picked on other children, because I was hurting or wanted the family they had. The disruptive behavior wasn't the only way being violated affected me. I struggled with my self-esteem, self-image and self-love. This also led to many more destructive behaviors. I eventually started to experiment with drugs and developed a cocaine addiction. I struggled with promiscuity and overeating, which were ways of further victimizing myself. These were outward manifestations of being molested and raped. The foul touch of the predators who traumatized me, frightened me. I was scared deep in my soul. Being violated in that way, skewed my perception of myself, my life and how I thought people saw me. The strength and hope to overcome my past came through my relationship with the triune God. Being in a personal relationship with Christ made it clear to me that I could not move forward, until I acknowledged and addressed what happened in my past.

Chapter 3

The Year of Manifestation

In those days Hezekiah became mortally ill; and he prayed to the LORD, and the LORD spoke to him and gave him a sign.
~ 2 Chronicles 32:24

The journey of dealing with my past began while I was attending a church whose theme for that particular year was The Year of Manifestation. The members were asked to write down three things we wanted God to manifest in our lives. I wrote that I wanted to be debt free, to lose weight and to be married again. I prayed all year for God to manifest these three things in my life. However, many of you know that when you ask God for something, things will often get messier before they get better? I sincerely prayed and truly wanted the things that I had written down to manifest in my life, but besides praying for the manifestation, I didn't make any changes. In my mind, as long as I prayed, God -- almost like a genie in a bottle -- would do everything I wrote down and I wouldn't have to do anything.

As the year went on, I had not noticed any changes in my weight, finances, or dating possibilities. In fact, things got worse. In June of that year, I was diagnosed with diabetes. I cried like a baby, when I found out. My doctor called me at work and said, "I called in a prescription to the Rite Aid for metformin. Take one a day, and you should get better." The only thing I could think of, was my limbs being amputated, injecting myself with insulin, being on dialysis and turning dark. I was an emotional wreck. In addition to being upset, I immediately became angry with my doctor for calling me with such bad news while I was at work. I told him how insensitive he was for calling me at work. I even went as far as changing my primary care doctor. I now realize that I was just taking my feelings out on him. I cried and ate for days. I made no attempt to change what I put into my body. I never looked at the part that I played in getting myself to a state, in which this was my diagnosis. I took the medicine and still ate carbs, fried foods, sweets and large amounts of food in one sitting. I just stuffed myself. I know now stuffing myself with food that was bad for me, was an indication of how much I was hurting. With my long history in social work, I never took the time to assess my own behaviors, despite working with people every day to help them better their lives.

The year was progressing. However, I was no closer to achieving any of the things I had written down in the beginning of the year. In September, my car was repossessed. Oh, the embarrassment I felt. I made up an elaborate lie about someone stealing my car. I couldn't believe that I had allowed my car to be taken from me. I started justifying my behavior, by saying, "That car was getting old anyway. I was paying too much. They can keep it!" Not once did I look at myself, my behavior, or my poor stewardship. Instead, I just continued praying for a financial breakthrough. Even when my prayers appeared to be falling on deaf ears and my life began to get messier, I continued to pray for God to send me help, so that I could live the life I deserved to live -- the blessed abundant life. I wanted God to bless my finances, but I would not tithe ten percent of my income, as God required. I gave, but it was not what the scriptures instructed us to pay.

One day, while I was talking to a friend about my dateless life, she suggested I sign up for an online dating site. I did. It was a disaster and I will never do that again. I met some nice people. However, I felt like I was settling, because I didn't have anything in common with many of them. We couldn't even have a decent conversation. I found that I was tolerating people, just to say I had someone. I dated people who had the potential to be something. That is not what I wanted. However, I know that the people I attracted were reflections of how I saw myself. I did not think well of myself during this time, so I accepted things that I should not have accepted. Thank the Lord, I have a better self-image now. I do not settle for any relationship, just for the sake of saying that I am in a relationship. I know deep in my heart how God feels about me.

Instead of seeking God and God's direction, all year I ran around trying to fill the void in my life with food, men, trips, clothes, and other unnecessary nonsense. On December 27, I was sitting on my couch, and tears began to fall down my face. I cried until my chest hurt. I was gasping for breath like a tearful child. The way I wept reminded me of how Hannah poured out her heart to God in the temple, until Eli thought she was drunk. I began to ask God why all these things happened that year and why nothing good manifested from my written prayers. I was a diabetic, did not have a car, my finances were jacked up and there was not even a potential husband in sight. I cried until I fell asleep.

God often speaks to me in my dreams, and this time was no different. "Daughter," I heard God speaking while I was asleep, "How can I bless your finances, if you won't return my tithe and trust me with your finances? How are you going to lose weight, if you eat anything that's not nailed down? (Well, he didn't say "anything that's not nailed down," but that's the gist of it.) Finally, how can I bless you with a husband, if you won't honor me with your body?" I was not wife material at that time. How could I submit to man, if I would not submit to God? Every area that was a problem for me required me to submit to God and to His word.

Although my prayers were not answered in the manner that I wanted them to be answered, the Lord revealed to me what I needed to be focused on and where I needed to grow. When I awoke, I said, "Okay, Lord, I hear you!" I then began to think of all the ways in which I needed to change. I couldn't do them all at one time, but I first decided to work on honoring God with my body. This seemed to be the most logical place to begin. I began to live a life of abstinence. I was pleased that I'd started to face my past and address my issues one at a time. This began my road to recovery.

Chapter 4

The Year of Revelation

I will cry out to God Most High, who accomplishes all things on my behalf for He completes my purpose in His plan.
~ Psalms 57:2

I began working on being abstinent, after God spoke to me through the dream. I would do well for a few weeks, then I would succumb to the temptation and end up fornicating again. it was awfully hard ignoring the late-night calls, text messages and pop-up visits. I would feel bad afterward, to the point of condemning myself. After a few days of feeling guilty, I'd give God the "I'm so sorry" speech and I'd try to manipulate God's word, by saying something like, "God, I don't want to burn in hell, but there's no husband in sight." When I reflect on some of my craziness, it's comical. I always eventually got back up and tried again. I was resisting as best I could on my own.

My breakthrough came when I attended a workshop entitled Break Every Chain at a women's conference. During the workshop, we were asked to write down on a card what stronghold we wanted God to break in our lives and why we thought it was a problem. We then put the 3x5 card in a makeshift coffin. While the song "Break Every Chain" played on repeat, I wrote, "I want to stop fornicating and honor God with my body. This is a problem for me, because I was raped at the age of nine." After everyone completed their cards, we began to line up, proceed toward the coffin and drop our cards in. It was very powerful to have a line of women walking to bury their hurts, shame, and struggles. We circled up to hold hands and pray. The power of God fell in the room. That was because we were all on one accord, touching and agreeing. I found myself on the floor in the corner crying and screaming out, "Lord, I don't want to live like that anymore." There was a release I felt in writing the real problem down. I felt a release in my spirit, when the prayer was over. I had to be ready spiritually to receive the healing God had for me.

James 5:16 says, "Therefore, confess your sins to each other and pray for each other so that you may be healed. The prayer of a righteous person is powerful and effective." That day, I experienced the truth and power in that scripture. It helped me through the healing process. After the prayer, I immediately found a minister to whom I could confess my sins. I explained what happened and that I needed someone to hold me accountable. We agreed to fast and pray for thirty days. I was finally on the road to recovery and to overcoming the ever so wrong touch that had traumatized me. In the beginning, it was a little difficult because I had to ignore the late-night phone calls. This may be a little too transparent for some people, but there was this one guy who I would see. He was like my "maintenance man." He kept calling and texting me so much, that I had to block him from calling my phone and delete him from my social media accounts. I was tempted more than once, but I always prayed for God's help and strength when I felt weak. I also would call the minister at times for prayer or just to talk about what I was feeling. I was at a place where I wanted to please God more than my flesh. It felt very empowering not to give in to the sexual urges.

Through abstinence, I began to heal from the abuse I had experienced. I started to regain my dignity, self-worth and self-respect. As I began to pray and draw closer to God, the Lord promised me that He would use every hurtful, harmful and shameful thing I had to endure for His glory. Yes, God was there with me when I was being abused. He was the one who protected my mind. Trouble must get God's approval. Just like with Job, satan had to ask God's permission to attack Job! God knew the day would come for me to deliver my testimony so that someone could be set free from their past. God is a healing God. He wants us to be free from all our baggage and bondage.

As I began the journey of healing through abstinence, it became clear how the wrong touch had caused so much turmoil in my life. I had to sit and unpack every way in which I had been affected by that wrong touch. Sitting quietly, journaling, analyzing and praying helped me begin to see myself as God saw me. I am the apple of His eye. I began to feel valuable, without someone else having to affirm me. Choosing to be celibate, if you are single, is the first step in the Come Out of the Ashes© Program.
Wow! With the help of God, I thought to myself, I can do this abstinence thing!

Part II

Road to Recovery

Chapter 5

Allow the Triune God into Your Situation

May the grace of the Lord Jesus Christ, and the love of God, and the fellowship of the Holy Spirit be with you all.
~ 2 Corinthians 13:14

I believe that God is three persons: God the Father; God the Son, who is Jesus; and God the Holy Spirit, who lives within us. This is what we call the triune God -- all three Gods in one.

While praying about getting free by breaking the chain of fornication from my life, the first revelation that I had was that, in order to succeed at the task, I needed help from God. I needed Him to work on the situation with me. I needed Him to give me strength and guidance on how to overcome my struggle. It was, therefore, important for me to build my relationship with the One who created me. I had been around church my entire life. I had served in many different capacities. I was a religious churchgoer, who lacked a true relationship with God. My real deliverance and healing happened, when I invited God into my daily life. I developed a relationship with Him as Abba Father, as Jehovah Rapha and the great I AM. In my healing process, I had to have faith and trust that God the Father could and would see me through. How did I build my relationship with God? My relationship with God was primarily developed through prayer, meditation and journaling. Through these practices, God revealed to me that in order not to fornicate and to remain abstinent, there were a few measures I needed to put in place.

First, I had to "date" God. For me, this meant that I had to end all romantic relationships and all conversations with men. I had to monitor the company I kept and the places I went. I had to guard my heart, if I was going to be successful at being abstinent. During this time, I remember leaving places if the conversation was of a sexual nature, closing my eyes like a little kid during movies or turning them off and blocking a few people on social media. Developing clear boundaries was very important during this time. I had to acknowledge that I could not make it or achieve healing without total dependence on God. It was a very lonely time, but it helped me mature spiritually. It helped my relationship with God to grow, and other relationships in my life were also mended during time. A major indicator of growth for me during that time was that I began to accept that I was different.

Building my relationship with God enabled me to learn how He sees me. I could always recite, "I am the apple of God's eye," but I was not living as the apple of his eye. I knew God's word said that I am fearfully and wonderfully made, but I didn't receive in my heart what that meant. When you know in your heart that you are the apple of God's eye and that you are fearfully and wonderfully made, you value yourself. You do not settle for anything less than God's best for yourself. You do not allow mistreatment from anyone, despite their title or position, for the sake of friendship, relationship, or status. I was so empowered during this time, that I removed myself from any situation which no longer suited who I was becoming.

Establishing my relationship with the God who created me in His image, helped me recognize that I am a daughter of the Most-High God. I embraced the truth that I am royalty and I accepted the responsibility to behave as such. God's word says in Genesis 1:26:

> Then God said, "Let Us [Father, Son, Holy Spirit] make man in Our image, according to Our likeness [not physical, but a spiritual personality and moral likeness]; and let them have complete authority over the fish of the sea, the birds of the air, the cattle, and over the entire earth, and over everything that creeps and crawls on the earth.

When I shifted my focus from performing religious acts to nurturing my relationship with God, is when I recognized that I was created in the image of God. That is when I knew that I had to rely on Him to help me heal. Once I understood that I am created in God's image and likeness, I knew that I was in the position to possess the freedom that God the Son offers. Unlike the old version of me, who grew angry and frustrated that my prayers alone were not enough to manifest the things that I asked God to give me, I now understood that for me to experience the freedom that Jesus references in John 8:36, required faith and work on my behalf. In order to experience godlike freedom, you first have to believe Jesus is the Son of God. In John 3:16, it says, "For God so loved the world that He gave His one and only Son, that whoever believes in Him will not perish but have eternal life."

Having faith and trusting in God is an essential part of overcoming trauma. There are several scriptures that show Jesus healing. He healed the lame, the blind, the dead, the woman with an issue of blood and the man with leprosy. Mark 1:40–42 says,

> A man with leprosy came to him and begged him on his knees, "If you are willing, you can make me clean." Jesus was indignant He reached out his hand and touched the man. "I am willing," he said. "Be clean!" Immediately the leprosy left him, and he was cleansed.

There was the nameless woman with the issue of blood, who pressed her way through a crowd, just to touch the hem of Jesus's garment. She crawled on her hands and knees to get to Jesus, because she did not have enough strength to stand. The mere fact that she risked her life shows the amount of desperation and faith she had. It demonstrates the lengths she was willing to go, to be healed. During this time, because she was continuously bleeding, she was considered unclean and could be killed, if she was in public. This is the type of faith it takes to heal from trauma! You have to be willing to press through what may feel like life threatening circumstances, be desperate to change and have great faith. You must decide to pursue your healing, despite people who block your way, obstacles and setbacks.

God is no respecter of persons. He doesn't play favorites. The same way He healed me, He will heal anyone who has the faith and is willing to pursue him. There are many examples of Jesus healing people with different types of issues in the Bible. The Bible points to Jesus and says that He is the way, the truth and the light. He died on the cross for our sins, shame and guilt, so that he could heal us from all of life's infirmities. In order to experience healing from the trauma you have suffered, you must have faith and be willing to pursue your healing by any means necessary. The Bible points us to Jesus. He is your Savior. Believe in Him. John 5:5 says, "Who is it that is victorious over (that conquers) the world but he who believes that Jesus is the Son of God?"

Just trust and have faith in God the Son. Jesus will heal your past and help you overcome your trauma. Seeing how Jesus healed people and wanting the same healing in my life was not always easy. It was hard at times to deny my flesh, when I had a desire to be with someone. I had to have an attitude of, For God I live, and for God I will die daily to my desires and know that God's way was the right way.

You are created in God's image. He sent Jesus, His son, to die on the cross for your sins, and you can be healed through Him of any ailment, sickness, disease or traumatic experience. Although Jesus is not here physically like He was with the early church, He left us the Holy Spirit. The Bible says, in John 14:15-17,

> *If you love me, keep my commands. And I will ask the Father, and He will give you another advocate to help you and be with you forever – the*

Spirit of truth. The world cannot accept him, because it neither sees Him nor knows Him. But you know Him, for He lives with you and will be in you.

As you begin to build your relationship with the triune God, you will want to please Him by keeping the commandments of Jesus, trusting and having faith in the power of the Holy Spirit to heal and utilizing the power within you to overcome your past. Building your relationship with God and trusting the process will prove to be very empowering and liberating, as you do the work it takes to move beyond the trauma of your past.

When we learn to believe in Christ and have faith in the word of God, we soon learn the decrees of God. The decrees of God are the promises of God. When you know the promises of God, you experience a peace that passes all understanding. You rest in the joy of the Lord and that joy makes you strong enough to get through the trying times that you will face on your path to overcoming your trauma. Trusting God with every part of your life, even the secret parts that you dare not tell anyone, will help you heal every single broken and damaged part of your soul. This is why cultivating a true relationship with Jesus Christ is the second step in the Come Out of the Ashes© process to healing trauma.

The Benefits of Loving God

Loving God in the way that I had grown to love and relate to Him had some other major benefits. In retrospect, building my relationship with God improved my relationships with the other people in my life. At one point in life, I was in conflict with everyone including: my family, colleagues, friends, and neighbors. However, after working on my relationship with God, I was able to live in peace with others. I watched damaged relationships mend. I really did not want to be this transparent, but by the prompting of the Holy Spirit, I felt that someone needed to hear my true testimony. For many years, I was angry with my mother because of my childhood and for all of the disappointment and pain I had experienced. Just the thought of the struggles in my life angered me. I felt that she could have done better. I wondered how she could not have known that I was being abused. It was not until I improved my relationship with God, that I realized that she did the best she could with the resources that were available to her at that time. I had to forgive her for what I thought she should have known. I had to look at the entire picture and was able to forgive her and accept her for who she was and not who I wanted her to be.

The freedom I gained from releasing my mother was like lifting an extremely heavy weight off me. In the end, I simply extended her the same grace that God extended to me. The ability to forgive and release the people and the pain of our past is a critical step in the process of overcoming trauma.

Chapter 6

Forgiveness

Bear with each other and forgive one another if any of you has a grievance against someone. Forgive as the Lord forgave you.
~ Colossians 3:13

Having great faith and enhancing your relationship with the triune God is how you lay the foundation to overcome trauma. The third step that you must take to begin to move past the trauma is to forgive. You must forgive your offender; the person who hurt you. You must forgive all non-offending or enabling parties, people who witnessed or knew about how you were violated but did not defend or rescue you and you must forgive yourself. Forgiveness like this takes success in the battle to heal from trauma, to a completely new level. Jesus taught about forgiveness in the book of Matthew 18:21-35 where it says,

> Then Peter came to Jesus and asked, "Lord, how many times shall I forgive my brother or sister who sins against me? Up to seven times?" Jesus answered, "I tell you, not seven times, but seventy-seven times. "Therefore, the kingdom of heaven is like a king who wanted to settle accounts with his servants. As he began the settlement, a man who owed him ten thousand bags of gold was brought to him. Since he was not able to pay, the master ordered that he and his wife and his children and all that he had be sold to repay the debt. "At this the servant fell on his knees before him. 'Be patient with me,' he begged, 'and I will pay back everything.' The servant's master took pity on him, canceled the debt and let him go. "But when that servant went out, he found one of his fellow servants who owed him a hundred silver coins. He grabbed him and

began to choke him. 'Pay back what you owe me!' he demanded. "His fellow servant fell to his knees and begged him, 'Be patient with me, and I will pay it back.' "But he refused. Instead, he went off and had the man thrown into prison until he could pay the debt. When the other servants saw what had happened, they were outraged and went and told their master everything that had happened. "Then the master called the servant in. 'You wicked servant,' he said, 'I canceled all that debt of yours because you begged me to. Shouldn't you have had mercy on your fellow servant just as I had on you?' In anger his master handed him over to the jailers to be tortured, until he should pay back all he owed. "This is how my heavenly Father will treat each of you unless you forgive your brother or sister from your heart."

The moral of the story is that Christians must extend the same grace to others, that God has extended to them. "Forgive and you shall be forgiven," is the word of God. Harboring ill feelings is not moving on, and not letting the trauma go is, in fact, keeping you stuck. Reliving the past repeatedly will never lead to healing. Forgiveness is not easy. We cannot forgive by our own strength, but God will give us the strength to forgive. Praying for someone who offended you, will help you to forgive. It is hard to stay mad at someone you're praying for daily. Forgiving someone does not mean you have to allow them the same access they had to your life before they hurt you. Letting go of the offense, while also putting boundaries in place to protect yourself, is necessary. When you forgive someone, you must remember Jesus's words to the disciples, when they were being promoted to apostles in Matthew 10:16. Jesus said, "I am sending you out like sheep among wolves. Therefore, be as shrewd as snakes and as innocent as doves."

Forgiveness has always been hard for me. In fact, I have struggled with forgiveness for most of my life. If someone offended or hurt me, I wouldn't seek revenge. However, I would act like they didn't exist, which was, at times, just as bad as if I had done something to get them back for what they had done to me. It wasn't until I began my journey of healing through abstinence, that I learned the importance of forgiveness. As I was drawing closer to God, He would just drop different people or situation in my heart and say, "It's time to let that go." This was a very powerful time in my journey. I know forgiveness can be a major challenge. Nonetheless, when you reflect during the healing process, you will also be led to forgive, because you will come to the realization that you have also offended and hurt people. God's grace is sufficient! God will give you the strength to forgive.

Forgiveness requires that we turn things over to God, and allow him to carry the burdens, hurts, offenses and betrayals that we have been carrying in our heart. Holding on to those feelings, only weighs you down. It is impossible to be free and move forward with unforgiveness in your heart. There are often lessons or teachable moments tucked within the very situations that hurt us. Instead of holding onto bitterness and unforgiveness, ask God what you are supposed to learn from the situation. There are a number of scriptures about casting our cares, problems and burdens on the Lord.

Give your burdens to the Lord. He will carry them. He will not permit the godly to slip or fall.

~ Psalms 55:22

Cast all your anxiety on Him because He cares for you.

~ 1 Peter 5:7

Forgiveness of self requires that you accept God's redemptive grace and love. Jesus was the sacrificial lamb that carried the weight of sin for you and me. There is nothing that can separate us from the love of God. Learning to forgive oneself and reflecting on God's redemptive grace and love can be overwhelming, when you get a glimpse of how He has guided your life and protected you in bad situations that could have been far worse. We must still accept the plans God laid before us as Christians. We will suffer like Christ. We don't have to like what happened to us, but we are commissioned to love our neighbors as we love ourselves. The truth is that because of our lack of love for self and our unaddressed trauma, some of us hate ourselves and are incapable of loving someone else. Hopefully, through the building of your relationship with God and the growth of your faith and trust in God, your evolving love of self will be inevitable.

God loves us dearly and deeply. Accepting His love and grace will produce self-love, self-acceptance and forgiveness of others. Those are the benefits of receiving the redemptive love of God. Redemptive love is more powerful than unconditional love because redemptive love restores you to your natural state of self -- before you sinned.

God's hand has been on me my entire life. God chased me down, until I surrendered to His will and His way. The freedom that I have found in God and from my past is indescribable. I forgave myself for not saying anything about being abused and I forgive my offenders. This journey has been very empowering and uplifting. However, it is a daily fight to stay in the right frame of mind.

Transforming your mind is the fourth step in the Come Out of the Ashes© process to overcoming trauma.

Chapter 7

Transform Your Mind

Do not conform to the pattern of this world but be transformed by the renewing of your mind. Then you will be able to test and approve what God's will is — his good, pleasing and perfect will.
~ Romans 12:2

Transforming your mind is a very difficult step, because the mind is the place that satan targets and attacks. We have established that overcoming trauma takes faith, trust and forgiveness. However, you cannot heal, if you continuously think about what happened to you. If you doubt that you can be healed, healing will not happen for you. As the scripture above tells us, we must renew our mind and renew it daily. At times, you may have to resort to renewing your mind on a minute by minute basis. If that is what you need to heal, then it is perfectly okay. As Christians, we are in the world but not of the world. We cannot do things like the world does them.

There needs to be a clearing of anything that distracts you from the love of God. In order to overcome trauma, you must renew your mind and turn your will and life over to Christ daily. You should concentrate on the good things in life, and do not dwell on negative experiences. If we are honest with ourselves, we learned something from the losses in our lives. Did I have to go through betrayal or being ridiculed to learn some of my life's lessons? Couldn't I have learned a different way? I probably could have. Nevertheless, the Lord uses everything to bring glory to His name and He uses the beautiful and broken places in our lives to grow and develop us.

One of the most important practices I have is my daily devotion. I dedicate the first few hours of my day to God. Having daily devotions sets the tone for the day. It puts me in a peaceful, positive mood. When I communicate with God consistently, I can often foresee trouble.

To transform your mind, you must monitor what you hear and what you see. Don't allow people to speak negatively to you or around you. It has been said that words have the power of life and death. Don't be surprised if, while on this journey of overcoming your trauma, you run into people who want to remind you of who you used to be. When I run into people from my past and they want to bring up an old story, I say things like, "Thank God for grace" or "God is so good." I shut it down instantly. Do not allow people's perception of you, to become your reality.

The apostle Paul tells us to think on the good, positive, pure and lovely things in life. God will give us His peace, if we keep our minds focused on Him. Overcoming trauma requires a renewing of the mind. When we change our thought patterns, it is almost like resetting the default button on your mind. It is very difficult to reprogram or change our way of thinking. However, it can be done. Consistency is the key.

In a portion of Proverbs 23:7 (King James Version) it says, "for as he thinketh in his heart, so is he:" However, if we go back to Proverbs 4:25-27, it says, "Let your eyes look straight ahead; fix your gaze directly before you. Give careful thought to the paths for your feet and be steadfast in all your ways. Do not turn to the right or the left; keep your foot from evil."

We are being warned to look straight ahead and keep our mind on Godly things. When Jesus told Peter to walk on the water, as long as Peter was focused on Jesus, he was not scared and did not sink. However, as soon as Peter took his eyes off Jesus, he began to get scared and sink. Our minds and gazes must be on what is directly ahead of us. Do not dwell on negative life experiences. Do not look back. Ask yourself, "What did I learn from the losses, disappointments, failures, traumas, betrayals and hurts of my past?" Do not dwell on what happened but do remember the lesson you learned and be steadfast in moving forward. We are what we think about most of the time. If we think we are defeated, then we will become defeated. We must have the mind of Christ, because the things we dwell on and allow to enter our minds become our reality.

Since I understand this, one of the things that I have incorporated into my program is daily affirmations. The daily affirmations begin with affirming who I am in God. I read them aloud to start my day positively. If I begin to feel insecure or if I am feeling down, I read my affirmations throughout the day. This is how my daily affirmations begin: For as a man thinketh in his heart, so is he! I am the apple of God's eye. I am fearfully and wonderfully made. I am the head and not the tail. I am above and not beneath. I am the lender and not the borrower!

It is important for me to remind myself daily of who I am as a child of God. This is because it is easy for me to fall into my old patterns of living and thinking. I had to change what I repeatedly told myself. I had to change what I thought about myself and what I thought about every day, so that I could create the life I wanted. I have been able to accomplish this, by doing mental check-ins and reflecting on my life.

Transforming our minds is not easy but it is necessary, and worth it, if we genuinely want to heal.

DELVIA BERRIAN

BEAUTY FOR ASHES

Chapter 8

Reflect to Stay on Track

I have considered my ways and have turned my steps to your statutes. I will hasten and not delay obeying your commands.
~ Psalms 119:59–60

As I shared in Chapter Seven, making the time for daily reflection is vital in the process of overcoming trauma and in helping us not to revert to old habits and ways of thinking.

Reflecting is a process, in which you ask yourself, "How am I doing?" It is a practice of regularly assessing yourself to make sure that nothing unusual has crept into your space or spirit. I have found out the importance of assessment and reflection the hard way—it was through another wrong touch. A few months after the writing of this chapter, I had two friends betray my trust. It was painful for me, because I considered them a part of my inner circle. They were my Peter, James, or John. When something great or bad happened in my life, I called them for a shoulder to cry on, to run things by and to get advice. The Holy Spirit will not allow you to be bamboozled. Psalms 25:14 says, "The LORD confides in those who fear him; he makes his covenant known to them."

The Lord will tell you His covenant and He will also warn you about the plan of the enemy. I was beyond hurt. These people betrayed my trust and they were close to me. However, as I stated earlier, God uses everything as a lesson. This betrayal taught me to closely monitor who I have in my circle. I cried for a long time about losing those friendships. However, their season in my life was over. God knew that I honor loyalty as a friend and that I would only have ended the relationships due to a lack of loyalty. I can honestly say that even before the betrayal, I saw signs that I needed to step away from these friendships. However, I did not pay attention. I failed to reflect, and I did not assess myself or the relationships in my life. This was a hard pill to swallow. Talk about forgiveness! These acts of betrayal tested my ability to forgive and challenged me to prove how much I trusted God. I wondered whether I could still show the love of Christ and interact with my Judas on a regular basis. This was a particularly challenging time for me. I would be lying, if I said it did not affect me. I believe the reason it affected me so much was because the person denied the offense, and never apologized. As a result, I decided to isolate myself and begin the process of healing trauma all over again.

You will find that when you are dealing with trauma, certain things trigger you. You will have certain common responses to those triggers. One of the signs that something is troubling me, is that I begin to snack or overeat.

Therefore, when I notice this behavior, I ask myself, "Hey, what's going on? Why are you overeating or snacking?" If I sit and reflect on what's been happening in my life, I can pinpoint what has upset me. After I identify the problem, I assess why is it bothering me. Is it something that I can address? Is it something out of my control? After I analyze the problem, I pray, and I turn it over to God. It is not always that easy. I may have to address some things a few times, because I'm human. However, I try to operate with faith in God, instead of my feelings. It is often a daily struggle to turn things over to God and not handle them myself. However, reflecting helps me to effectively process my disappointments.

It is very important to do self-checks to monitor the relationships in your life. This prevents you from slipping back into old habits and patterns. Reflections also help you to continue to develop your relationship with God. It wasn't until I began writing this book, that I realized I had fallen from my place of peace. I had to get the peace back in my life. When I reflected on my life, I had gained about fifteen pounds. I had started eating things I had stopped eating and was unsure of what my next step in life should be. This was a clear indication I had allowed distance to form in my relationship with God. I began praying for God to reveal to me what the root of the problem was and He did. I was harboring unforgiveness for the two people who had offended me. Although I thought I had given it over to God, I hadn't. I was still hurt. I expected more of these two individuals because I thought we were close. I used the same Come Out the Ashes© steps that I had used before, to heal from the hurt of my childhood. I had to settle myself, stay still and process those incidents, in order to get my peace back. I had to release and forgive them, even though they never apologized.

I added daily check-ins during my devotional time: "How are you doing today?" I always answer honestly. If I am discouraged, I identify why I feel discouraged and I intentionally address the discouragement with the word of God. If I feel lonely, I fill the loneliness with the word of God. I want you to do the same. As stated from the very beginning, what has been the major healing factor of my trauma during this journey, has been my relationship with the triune God! Do you remember the process I designed and followed once I decided to gain freedom from my past? We will review steps seven and eight in the next two chapters. Let's review the process:

Come Out of the Ashes©: 7-Step Process to Healing Trauma

1. Abstain from Sex (if you are not married)
2. Cultivate Your Relationship with Jesus Christ
3. Forgive your Offenders and Forgive Yourself
4. Transform Your Mind
5. Reflect Daily
6. Walk in Your Purpose
7. Keep a Journal

The God who created us, the God who shed His blood for our sins, and God the Spirit who walks with us and guides us every day is with us. Know what your triggers are and reflect every day and you will greatly prevent the regressions that will otherwise occur in your life.

Chapter 9

Walk in Purpose

"For I know the plans I have for you," declares the LORD, *"plans to prosper you and not to harm you, plans to give you hope and a future."*
~ Jeremiah 29:11

When I wrote that I wanted to be debt free, lose weight and marry again, those were the three things I wanted God to manifest in my life. I never imagined that my prayer requests would lead me to turn the process I went through to heal my childhood trauma, into the Come Out of the Ashes© program. I also certainly never expected that I would write a book! The fact that the prayer requests that I wrote down brought about a deeper relationship with God and healing in my life is amazing. I would be lying if I said the road has been easy and I have not gotten all of the things I prayed for yet, but I can say without a doubt that I am at peace. I restored and deepened my relationship with God, and I am not the same person who filled out that prayer request card in church that day. God had a purpose for me.

My story reminds me of Joseph, the dreamer. Did he think his grand dreams would lead to him ending up in a pit, in Potiphar's house and in prison? I'm sure he did not. There are countless stories of God's hand being on people's lives through adverse circumstances. Elijah, David, Job, and many more people in the Bible are examples of just that. It is just like Joseph told his brothers, "What you all meant for evil, God used for His good," I believe God has used and is using my story to impact His kingdom on the earth. There is no doubt in my mind the Lord has set me apart to help empower and encourage not just women, but anyone who has experienced any kind of trauma. God did not save me and deliver me to keep my story to myself. He wants the same thing for you. With God, all things are possible. He is a healer. It is the very thing that was sent to break you and me and keep us from fulfilling our destinies. God is using it for his glory. God knew, before I was born, that I would help people overcome their trauma. He knew when I was the angry little girl and that I would go on to help other angry little girls and boys. He also knows what good you will do for others, once you heal from your trauma.

There are many people struggling with their childhood trauma, because they have not invited God into their situations. As a healthcare professional, I have participated in several therapeutic workshops and conferences. I have read and completed professional development on everything from self-help groups to individual therapy. I have been exposed to and even tried it all. However, nothing worked, until I turned everything over to God. Some of the methods did help, but I found that many of the processes conflicted with God's word. Seek Christian counseling that is based on God's word and on Christian principles.

As Christians, we must be able to adapt to what life throws at us. Our faith and hope should be in God. God sent his Son, Jesus, that we might have a right to the tree of life. He wants us to live lives of freedom and not bondage. Christ died on the cross to take on our guilt, shame, pain, and every hurtful thing that we have had to endure. I made a conscious decision not to allow my past to dictate my future. The word of God encourages us to trust in God. Of course, I wish my childhood was different, but would I have had the awesome assignment of helping those who are burdened with the guilt and shame of sexual abuse to overcome it, if I had not experienced what I did as a child ? I am not sure. I am positively honored, however, that God trusts and uses me to guide others through the healing process. I am honored that God trusts me with this assignment.

As Christians, we must aim to be transformed into the image of Christ who gave us an example of how to live. He left us here on earth as living sacrifices. We are to be a model for the world to show them that Jesus is the way, the truth and the light. When Jesus healed various people in the Bible, they were given different instructions. Some were told to tell no one, and others who received healing were told to go and tell everyone what Jesus had done for them. Stay connected to God and He will reveal your purpose, so that you can fulfill it. He will show you how to use your story to help somebody else.

DELVIA BERRIAN

Chapter 10

Keep a Journal

And the Lord answered me, and said, Write the vision, and make [it] plain upon tables, that he may run that readeth it.
~ Habakkuk 2:2

Earlier in the book, we established the multiple values of reflecting and journaling. I also shared how I used both reflecting and journaling to heal from the trauma of my childhood, as well as from some of the difficult situations that I faced in my adulthood.

There are several stages of healing from trauma. The fact you picked up this journal is a sign that you are contemplating making a change. This chapter is designed to serve as your kickstart Come Out of the Ashes© journal. Using this journal will help you grow deeper in your relationship with God and have a better understanding of who you are, your purpose and the plan God has for your life.

God wants you to live a free and abundant life! Take some time to reflect and journal now.

Come Out of the Ashes© Starter Journal

1. What is your story?

_____
_____
_____
_____
_____
_____
_____
_____
_____
_____
_____

2. How have you seen God's hand in your story?

_____
_____
_____
_____
_____
_____
_____

3. What most shaped you into the person you are today?

_____
_____
_____
_____
_____
_____
_____
_____
_____
_____

4. What are the experiences that most impacted you? List both the positive and the negative.

_____
_____
_____
_____
_____
_____
_____
_____

5. Do you think you can you use your story to help someone else? Why or why not?

_____
_____
_____
_____
_____
_____
_____
_____

6. Are there things you would like God to manifest in your life? List them and begin to pray that God will reveal to you what actions you

need to take, in to order receive what you prayed for.

7. Honestly evaluate your relationship with God. What can you do to improve your relationship with God?

8. In what areas of your life have you chosen not to give God access?

_____
_____
_____
_____
_____
_____
_____
_____

9. How do you handle offenses?

_____
_____
_____
_____
_____
_____
_____
_____
_____
_____

10. How easily do you forgive? Is there room for improvement?

_____
_____
_____
_____
_____
_____
_____
_____

11. List the name(s) of the people you need to forgive.

_____
_____
_____
_____
_____
_____
_____
_____
_____
_____
_____

12. Create a daily affirmation to help you maintain a positive self-image and to boost your self-esteem.

_____
_____
_____
_____
_____
_____
_____
_____

13. Make an honest assessment of yourself. How do you feel about your life and work? Do you need to make any changes?

_____
_____
_____
_____
_____
_____
_____
_____

14. Have you discovered your God-given purpose?

_____
_____
_____
_____
_____
_____
_____
_____

15. Are you walking in your purpose? Explain how.

_____
_____
_____
_____
_____
_____
_____
_____

16. What do you need to do to fulfill God's purpose for your life?

_____
_____

_____
_____
_____
_____
_____
_____

17. What are some of the things that interfered or that could interfere with God's plan for your life?

_____
_____
_____
_____
_____
_____
_____
_____

18. What is the root of your trauma?

_____
_____
_____
_____
_____

19. Identify what blocks you from getting free. Is it unforgiveness or anger toward God for unanswered prayers, etc.

20. There are times in our lives when God is stretching us, by removing the dead things. What is God asking you to turn away from or let go?

BEAUTY FOR ASHES

_____
_____
_____
_____
_____

DELVIA BERRIAN

Part III

A Trauma Workers Survival Guide

What I have Learned from my Trauma and from Working with People in Trauma

Chapter 11

A Trauma Workers Survival Guide

Let everything you do be done in love motivated and inspired by God's love for us.
~ 1 Corinthians 16:14

This chapter is dedicated to those who encounter people in their profession who have experienced trauma. This includes the child welfare worker, teacher, counselor, youth worker or pastor. To effectively treat someone who has been abused or suffered from some form of trauma you must use the following approaches and styles in your practice. I have found that using these strategies fosters successful therapeutic relationships and leads to more positive results for the client and the professional.

Servant Leadership Leads to Success

It is important to use the servant leadership approach and to be an empathetic listener. The servant leadership approach is about having a servant attitude. It is a humble approach that allows for introspection and builds trust. We should not come across as dictators in our service to our clients.

What do I mean by servant? We are paid (or you have volunteered) to provide a service to people in need. Although you may be in a position of authority or leadership, if you really open your mind, you are there to serve and to help. Operating from this approach requires us to take on the character of Christ -- a humble servant. As a humble servant, you will encourage, be compassionate, empathetic, have integrity and demonstrate authenticity and transparency. All of these servant leadership qualities are needed to reach a person who has suffered the trauma of abuse. This is because these individuals are often extremely distrustful and guarded. Therefore, it takes a very patient, genuine and understanding person to encourage them to remove the barriers they built up to protect themselves from years of abuse and pain.

Servant leadership actually empowers the people we serve. Jesus showed great humility, by washing the feet of his disciples. If Jesus can humble Himself to serve, why can't we as professionals humble ourselves to serve the people God entrusts to us? Showing humility is sometimes seen as a sign of weakness. However, it is a strength. Being humble is being willing to learn. It means choosing not to work with the attitude that you know everything.

Let the people you are working with tell you what their issues, concerns or traumatic experiences are. Do not fall into the trap of assuming that their trauma is the same as the last person's trauma. Everyone deals with trauma differently.

When you allow your client to voice how the trauma that they survived impacted them, you use what we call collaborative authority. This empowers the people we work to help. Collaborative authority promotes teamwork, respect and the equitable distribution of power. This use of authority also helps, when it comes to evaluating results. This approach works well within many settings. However, within the child welfare system, where clients are often forced to work with social workers instead of being able to choose who they work with, relating to the client can be especially difficult. With the servant leadership approach, however, you can also even win over the clients who are court mandated.

As a social worker for the Department of Human Services (DHS), I had clients who had court mandated services. They could have been mandated, because they were uncooperative due to truancy or for a variety of reasons. Whatever the reason was, these clients were often the most difficult to help, because they did not want to be bothered. As far as they were concerned, the services were an intrusion for them. I specifically remember a mother who was mandated for services. I can't recall why she was mandated, but her terrible attitude is still fresh in my mind. This woman was very disrespectful. She called me names and was always unavailable for joint meetings. She had no problem meeting and cooperating with the provider agency. Her issue was with DHS, which meant her issue was with me. I managed to turn this difficult relationship around. One day when we were in court, the judge wanted to place her children in foster care, because of the persistent issues in her home. I asked the judge to give her another few months, to correct the issues and agreed that if the situation was not better at the next court appearance, to place the children at the bar of the court. She was still uncooperative, but not totally uncooperative. She worked well with the in-home services provider just not DHS – not with me. After we left the courtroom, the mother was still very rude. We had a brief meeting after the hearing, where I outlined what needed to take place in order for the court to be discharged and what she needed to take care of, in order for DHS to be out of her life for good. When I met with the mother at our next appointment, which was at the mom's house, her attitude was much better. She wasn't overly nice, but neither was she rude or disrespectful. I eventually helped her to get some new beds and school supplies for the children and put other supports in place to assist her with providing for her family. The year the case was set to close, the mom hugged me and was crying. I showed the mother that I was on her side. No matter what, I was there to serve her and her children. Although she was disrespectful, I did not take it personally. In the end, her entire family was better off because of the approach I decided to take with her.

Those who work with people in trauma, often take the disrespect and attitudes of those they work with personally. This is because we are the targets for their anger. It is important to rethink this. We must have the heart and mind of Christ. Do not retaliate and make things more difficult for them. You are there to serve. Just try to empathize with how they feel. Their actions are wrong, but you are the professional. You are the helper and you should never resort to spiteful tactics.

Utilizing the servant leadership perspective also requires you to be aware of your biases. When working with someone who has experienced sexual abuse, it is important for you to be self-aware and know your biases, be aware of your shortcomings, issues and convictions and understand that you can have a negative impact on someone if you are not working from a healthy space mentally.

Statistics indicate that people who have been abused often display self-destructive behaviors or they become threats to others. The abused, in effect, becomes the abuser. Due to the specific type of trauma I endured, even if the abuser was abused themselves, clients who sexually abuse children are the most difficult population for me to work with. As professionals, we must know ourselves enough to be honest and to operate in integrity. To say, "I won't be able to help this person, because I have not gotten past this issue personally," is the responsible and professional thing to do.

To be clear, I have empathy for those who have had traumatic experiences similar to mine.

However, I also know when I can or cannot help them. It depends on the situation and on where I am emotionally at that point in my life. When we don't decline opportunities that may trigger our own trauma, we are not helping the process for anyone. Holding on to clients, congregants or whoever you are working to help, when you are not truly well enough to work with them, can only do more harm than good.

When you have experienced trauma, you are often acutely intuitive when it comes to people's character. When I am in tune with myself, I can tell if someone is really for me or not. This is known as the fight or flight mode, which is a physiological reaction to stress or danger. Although there may not be a real danger, if clients perceive danger because of a disingenuous approach, they will not be able to heal through that interaction. Naturally, we don't want to admit our shortcomings because we all have egos. I've heard it said that when we let our ego get in the way, we are edging God out. Help people heal. Allow God into the relationship and move out of the way, if you cannot help the person.

In some instances, such as in DHS, giving a case to someone else, when the assigned social worker is struggling with a bias or a trigger, may not be an option. In those cases, it is your job to make your supervisor aware of your challenge, so that he or she can coach you through the case and hold you accountable for serving the client well. This requires patience and honesty from both parties involved. The supervisor must be willing to question every decision made by the case worker and ask for clarity, when needed. The social worker must make themselves accountable and accept emotional support as needed, so they can grow professionally. These types of situations require the social worker to face their trauma head on. If we are going to be agents of positive change, we must change. That is how we improve as individuals, families and communities, one person at a time.

Keep Care Client-Centered

It is important that we meet our clients where they are in the healing process. This is called client-centered treatment – an approach that allows the client to take an active role in their treatment. The approach increases the self-esteem of the person you are working with, and also brings about self-awareness. It empowers them to take charge of their destiny and to avoid adapting a victim mindset. For example, when you encounter someone who is still in the self-destructive phase of their trauma, how do you approach them from a client-centered perspective? Most of all, communicating with them from a non-judgmental point of view is essential. The hope is that, with time, patience and strategic care, the client will experience an internal motivation to do the work that is required, in order for them to change.

Because this book is based on biblical principles and my approach to healing is strongly based on establishing and nurturing a relationship with God, assuring clients of Romans 8:1 brings great comfort and hope. The scripture says, "There is therefore now no condemnation to them which are in Christ Jesus, who walk not after the flesh, but after the Spirit." Although they may currently be engaging in destructive behavior, pray for and (if you can) pray with your client. Show them how to accept Jesus into their life and how to create an environment that promotes growth in their Christian walk. Getting them started with the 7-step Come Out of the Ashes© process will help.

    I have gone to therapy several times to address various life experiences. I once hired a therapist to help me process the trauma of being betrayed. This therapist was not a Christian therapist, but she had been in practice for several years. I had used her when I was going through my divorce, so I chose to go with her again. It is important for me to note that one of the disadvantages of doing therapy as someone in the social work or counseling profession, is that they are analyzing you as you are analyzing them. It's inevitable and my experience was no different. I told the therapist that I had two people who were very near and dear to my heart betray me. I talked about how the experience made it hard for me to trust again and explained that I saw myself superimposing that distrust into new relationships. We had a major disagreement on the issue. She wanted me to confront the two people who had broken my trust. However, I disagreed because I was in a professional relationship with one of the people and I did not want to mix my emotions with that relationship. I did not want to confront the other person, because I had already given them an opportunity to discuss what happened and they denied doing anything wrong. Therefore, I felt that it was useless to rehash the matter with them. This therapist knew that I was a Christian. Her response was very unprofessional and personal. When I explained I was not going to confront either person, and I told her why, she said, "If the Bishop told you to go to them, would you?" She knew that I followed this particular clergy person and read many of their books on healing. I felt that her response was a criticism of my belief system. I answered that, "I would have to ask his reason for telling me to confront them." Needless to say, after that exchange, I decided that she could not help me. I no longer felt comfortable with her, because she did not make those sessions a safe place for me to work through my feelings. She also judged me. Had she used a client-centered approach, she would have allowed me to work through my feelings, accepted my reasons for disagreeing with her suggestions and supported my decisions.

These three approaches are about service, humility, self-care and promoting growth and healing for anyone who is in your service. For some of the reasons I shared, applying these strategies may not work for all therapeutic relationships. However, if there is going to be any level of trust and progress made in the lives of the hurting people we work to help, we need to at least be aware of these three approaches, so that we can use them as often as possible.

Empathetic Listening

Another effective approach for professionals to use when helping people work through trauma is empathetic listening. Listening in this way requires that we shift our thinking from trying to be understood or have our solutions and advice understood, to putting the other person's needs before everything. People want to know that you care about them and that you are concerned about their well-being. As a person who can be highly competitive, task driven and overly organized, I often have to take a step back from being paperwork and numbers driven. We must stop pushing our agendas, which could, for example, be to complete an investigation, finish an assignment or just get to the next thing on our to-do-list. We need to take time to understand the person sitting in front of us. It is easy to miss what is really going on with clients, when we are too focused on getting to the next assignment. As a trained social worker, the skill of listening is always a good trait to have, especially when leading abuse investigations. You must be able to listen for what is said and what is not said. If you truly utilize the technique of empathetic listening to understand your clients, you will create relationships in which compassion and trust begins to develop in the relationship. Building trust is like peeling layers off of an onion. The more you listen, the more you learn about your clients.

To be understood by someone is therapeutic. Your clients, congregants or whoever you serve, will appreciate that you pay attention to their feelings, listen for queues from them about particular areas of importance and seek to gain perspective on the problems. You also become vulnerable, when you chose to be an empathetic listener. Consequently, professionals, have to be careful not to take on their client's emotions. Taking on the pain of the client can lead to vicarious trauma. When you have been working with people who have experienced trauma, it can become overwhelming. This can easily result in burn out. As professionals, we must protect ourselves and practice self-care, in order to prevent compassion fatigue and vicarious traumatization. In order to keep healthy boundaries, it is important to be self-aware, tune into your own feelings and make self-care a priority.

Afterword

The Spirit of the Lord is on me, because he has anointed me to proclaim good news to the poor. He has sent me to proclaim freedom for the prisoners and recovery of sight for the blind, to set the oppressed free.

~ Luke 4:18

My brothers and sisters, there is a balm in Gilead to heal the broken places in your life. When you allow God to heal you, He will heal you from the very core of your being. This only happens when you are open and honest with God about your thoughts and your feelings. God already knows how you feel. He just wants you to confess your feelings to Him. You may feel angry and question God about the trauma you experienced. Pray about the anger honestly. To stay stuck in the anger, is to assume the role of victim. A victim is someone who suffers from a destructive act. Yes, you were a victim of a horrible violation. Maybe your trauma lasted for a long period of time. You are the only one knows the gravity of what you experienced and how it made you feel. However, you don't have to stay there. Come Out of the Ashes! You don't have to remain a victim. You do not have to allow your trauma to control you or to determine your destiny. God wants to make a trade with you – His beauty for your ashes.

I dare you to give all the pain, guilt, shame, anger and fear to God. It's not easy to deal with trauma. No one can force you to address the trauma, until you're ready. I attended a church where they were beginning a sexual survivor's ministry. It was a great way to help people who suffered abuse, However, let me tell you, I avoided this ministry like the plague! I was just not ready to deal with my trauma. I had lived in victim mode for so long, that I had suppressed what happened to me. I forgot about what happened, and at the same time, I lived with the residue of the trauma every single day. The angry little girl I was, had grown into an angry woman who would tell you off in a hot minute and stir up all kinds of drama. I was just messy. I was a person in pain doing everything to fill a void. I shopped excessively and tried to create an image of a person who had it all together, but I was hurting inside. I was a people-pleasing person, who was doing everything to make friends. I knew that many of them didn't have my best interest at heart. However, I was searching for love in all the wrong people and in all the wrong places.

Does any of this sound like what you do? Are you covering up your hurt and pain with things? Let God into your trauma and He will give you freedom from the wrong that was done to you.

It is not easy to change. It is very uncomfortable, but with the power of God helping you, you can do it. He wants to heal the wounded child inside of you. It is okay to grieve what you lost. You may have lost the privilege of feeling safe. You may feel guilt, shame, or fear. You may regret the choices that were made for you. One of the things I would get most angry about, was that I didn't lose my virginity to the person of my choice. That is a big deal, even to teenagers who grow up in church and are taught that sex outside of marriage is wrong. I could never relate to my friends, when they talked about their first experiences. I had to get to a place where I realized that the trauma was not my fault. Your trauma is not your fault. Stop questioning what you could have done differently and begin to show compassion for yourself. Speak to yourself, when negative thoughts arise. This is when the daily affirmations are good to use, because they remind you of who you are in Christ Jesus. When you accept that you are God's most precious possession, then you will begin to walk in the freedom that God gave you.

After I began to address my character flaws, I was better able to deal with my trauma. Surviving trauma can be just that -- surviving. I began to take back some of my power. I no longer allowed what happened to me control me. I began to stop trying to please people. I started to accept my story and work on myself from a holistic perspective. I had to make an honest assessment of who I was and how I was doing. Surviving, for me, was being the walking wounded. I was accomplishing things in life, but was I was not really living my best life – which is a free life. I was still bound.

Don't get me wrong, I was changing. However, I was also still living with some of the residue of being abused. I know that I will never be perfect, but I was still allowing the trauma to control how I saw myself. I was bound, because I had not yet made peace yet with my trauma, myself or my offenders. However, the instant that I honestly turned everything that I struggled with over to God, I felt a release. I began to see myself through the eyes of God. I spent time in His presence and learned how much God loved me. I came to understand how much He was concerned about me. When that happened, the enemy could no longer consume me with drugs, sexual or physical abuse, poverty, or anything else that He threw my way, because I had learned that with the power of God, I could overcome anything.

God is concerned about you. The word tells you in 1 Peter 5:7 to cast your cares on God, because He cares for you. Spend time in God's presence, turn every hurt and pain over to Him. I promise you. He will make things clear for you.

Remember, that God uses the least likely people to do the most amazing things! People will try to keep you locked into who you used to be. I see it all the time, but we all evolve. Don't allow people to keep you stuck at who you used to be. When we look at the life of Joseph, we see how much he suffered. Who would believe that he would become the prince of Egypt and would be the one who'd eventually save his family?

Look at Esther, who was strategically placed in the house of King Xerxes to help the Jews. Given that she was a Jew, she should never have been in the position of Queen. The king's advisor, Haman, got permission from the king to have all the Jews in the kingdom killed. However, Esther stopped the plan of Haman and the king had Haman hung on the very pole he had set up for Mordecai to be killed on. Esther was placed in a position to help her people and spare their lives.

The Apostle Paul was the greatest persecutor of Christians. He was a part of the crowd who stood by when Stephen was stoned. He hated people of "the way" (as was said of

Christians back then) but look how God used him. He was used to write most of the New Testament. God wants to use you to help His people. How He wants to use you, I am not sure, but He will show you. The negative things that happened to me could have crushed anyone's hopes and dreams. However, in the end, it was all a part of God's divine plan to get me to the place to write and publish this book. I was supposed to help you overcome the trauma of your past. Nothing I've been through and nothing you've been through will be wasted. You must know that God will use it all for His glory. He will use it to heal His people and expand His kingdom. Believe and have faith in Him, and fight through the pain, shame, fear and guilt. There is a balm in Gilead to heal you!

I would be lying, if I said it was easy for me to write this book. I found myself going through some of the pain, shame and hurt again, because I knew what scrutiny this type of transparency could bring. At one point during this process, I noticed myself overeating again and had to ask myself, "What's going on with you, that your stuffing yourself? What is it that you are not addressing?" I stopped. I went through my seven steps and figured it out. I needed to address how was going to deal with it, when people began to talk about what I had written. I took that to God in prayer. I trust God! Trust God with your fears and your doubts. God will take care of everything. This process is a lifelong process, because anything can trigger your old survival habits. Find someone you can talk with honestly and openly about the trauma that you endured. Sometimes the only person we'll be able to talk with about it all is God, because not everyone can relate. The good news is that, He is a safe place to dump everything that's happening in your mind and heart. Trust the process and let Him help you Come Out of the Ashes!

DELVIA BERRIAN

About the Author

Delvia Y. Berrian is a native of Philadelphia, Pennsylvania. She is a graduate of Temple University College of Public Health School of Social Work. She earned her Bachelor's and Master's degrees in Social Work. She also earned a Master's degree in Theological Studies from Palmer Theological Seminary.

Delvia has served as a child welfare advocate for nearly three decades.

Delvia is a woman after God's heart. She is known for her many acts of kindness and for her dedication to improving the lives of children and youth. It has always been her passion to inspire women and girls to strive to reach their greatest potential.

Delvia is the founder of PRESS for Kingdom Living, an organization committed to empowering young girls and women. Her goal is support them by offering workshops, coaching and other events that help them to live God-fearing lives, while overcoming life's challenges. Ultimately, she wants to see women catapulted into their God-given purposes.

www.ingramcontent.com/pod-product-compliance
Lightning Source LLC
Chambersburg PA
CBHW070923160426
43193CB00011B/1562